I'M GOOD AT
MUSIC
WHAT JOB CAN I GET?

Richard Spilsbury

WAYLAND

First published in 2013 by Wayland
Copyright © Wayland 2013

Wayland
338 Euston Road
London NW1 3BH

Wayland Australia
Level 17/207
Kent Street
Sydney, NSW 2000

Produced for Wayland by
White-Thomson Publishing Ltd
www.wtpub.co.uk
+44 (0)843 2087 460

Editor: Kelly Davis
Designer: Tim Mayer
Picture research: Richard Spilsbury
Proofreader and indexer: Lucy Ross

Dewey categorisation: 780.2'3-dc23

ISBN-13: 9780750280075

Printed in China

10 9 8 7 6 5 4 3 2 1

Wayland is a division of Hachette
Children's Books, an Hachette UK company.
www.hachette.co.uk

Picture credits

1. Dreamstime/Globephoto; 3. Dreamstime/Darrinhenry; 4. Dreamstime/Aijadream; 5. Dreamstime/Creatista; 6. Dreamstime/Farek; 7. Dreamstime/Ayessemedia; 8. Dreamstime/Pcruciatti; 9. Dreamstime/Jackc61; 10. Dreamstime/Arim44; 11. Dreamstime/Newsfocus1; 12 Shutterstock/Salim October; 13. Dreamstime/Avava; 14. Shutterstock/antb; 15. Dreamstime/Darrinhenry; 16. Dreamstime/ Imageegami; 17. Dreamstime/Karimala; 18. Dreamstime/Sbukley; 19. Dreamstime/Yuri Arcurs; 20. Dreamstime/Aliakosta; 21. Dreamstime/Luckybusiness; 22. Dreamstime/Feverpitched; 23. Dreamstime/Isaiahlove; 24. Shutterstock/stockyimages; 25. Shutterstock/s_bukley; 26. Dreamstime/Globephoto; 27. Dreamstime/Dmitrimaruta; 28. Dreamstime/7artman; 29. Shutterstock/Diego Cervo; cover (top left), Shutterstock/Alan Heartfield; cover (top right), Shutterstock/Kruglov_Orda; cover (bottom), Shutterstock/Maxim Blinkov.

Disclaimer

The website addresses (URLs) included in this book were valid at the time of going to press. However, it is possible that contents or addresses may have changed since the publication of this book. No responsibility for any such changes can be accepted by either the author or the Publisher.

CONTENTS

The world of music

Imagine life without music. Musical expression has always been an important part of human life. Every culture in the world today makes music, and musical instruments are among the oldest man-made objects ever found.

PROFESSIONAL VIEWPOINT

'I think to get into the music industry, you've got to be prepared to work really hard. I did years of work experience, working free for magazines and record labels. Anything to get a foot in the door, meet the right people, make the right contacts, and do something different.'

Rob Da Bank, DJ and music producer

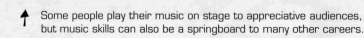
Some people play their music on stage to appreciative audiences, but music skills can also be a springboard to many other careers.

The importance of music

Music is a universal language. It inspires feelings and thoughts, and can express emotions without the need for words. However, a melody and rhythms can also focus attention on words in songs, and emphasise emotions or events depicted, say, in a film. Musical creations can help people enjoy and view the world in a new way. Music bridges gaps between cultures, bringing people together and creating a community.

Music in the workplace

Musical ability is useful in a wide range of jobs, not just in bands and orchestras. Music is used in advertising and marketing, in films and documentaries, in stage shows (such as musicals, plays and ballets), in schools, in the soundtracks for video games, and in many other professions.

➡

Some sitar players are specialist musicians who often play Indian music for live performances or film scores.

Special skills

Playing music uses many brain functions at the same time: motor control, imagination, hearing, sight and memory. Someone who is good at music has a lot of technical and creative skills that are transferable to many jobs. They are inventive and usually self-disciplined and self-motivated, as they have to practise and complete work on their own. It is a competitive field and you need skill and determination to make a career in music but it can be very satisfying. Read on to find out about some of the career paths you could follow.

Musician

Musicians are creative artists. They play in bands or as solo artists, as session musicians or in orchestras. They sing, or play one or more instruments, live and in recording studios.

An orchestral musician contributes to a rich, multi-layered performance of music that often requires great technical skill.

What skills do I need?

You will need drive, patience, persistence and dedication to be a musician. Most professional musicians practise and rehearse daily for hours they are not paid for directly, to improve their skills and get work. Many of them perform in the evenings and at weekends. Some pop musicians become professional after forming bands or promoting their work at live gigs and on the Internet. Others may study diplomas or A-levels in music or performance at school or college. Most classical musicians attain high standards in music performance and theory exams to attend specialist music colleges, and then audition to join orchestras or other groups.

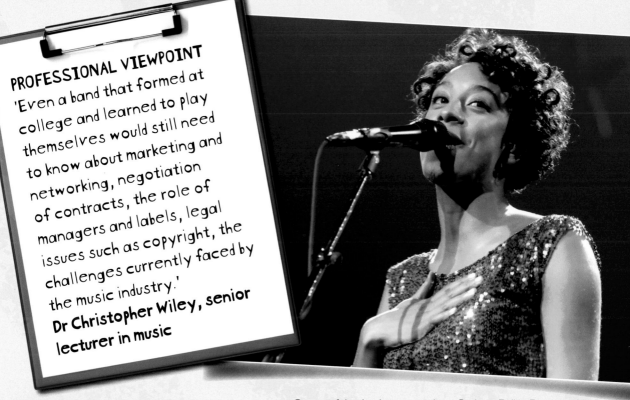

▲ Successful solo singers, such as Corinne Bailey Rae, combine musical skills with personality and stage presence.

Different types of musician

Church organist, concert violinist and multi-instrumentalist in a theatre band are just a few examples of types of musician. Some compose and play their own work, while others play compositions written by other musicians. Some are salaried members of one ensemble; others are freelancers working for several groups. Most musicians specialise in a particular musical genre, such as jazz or bluegrass, while others (such as session musicians) might play many genres for different jobs. Some musicians tour the world playing, but others always play near where they live.

Job description

Musicians:
- perform in concerts and in recording sessions
- practise regularly and learn new pieces of music
- prepare for auditions, rehearsals and performances
- maintain and tune/set-up their instrument(s), amplifiers and other equipment
- promote their music and skills, and negotiate performance and recording fees
- seek out and liaise with music managers and new performance venues.

7

Festival promoter

Have you experienced the buzz of being at a big music festival? Imagine the excitement of organising a festival and promoting the acts that make it a success. Festival promoters set up, publicise and manage live music events.

Job description

Festival promoters:
- research and choose suitable acts for the intended audiences
- liaise with musicians and agents to negotiate fees and schedule performances
- find and book existing venues and source suppliers of staging, catering and lighting
- co-ordinate and arrange a full programme of gigs for the festival
- organise publicity in a variety of media, from posters to radio interviews
- liaise with broadcasters and filmmakers to show festival performances.

→ Promoters get great job satisfaction from seeing their musicians perform in front of large festival crowds.

What skills do I need?

Organising and running a festival takes drive and persistence. You will need excellent spoken and written communication skills to persuade bands to appear at a festival and to attract an audience. Promoters need to be well-organised and able to work under pressure. Some take a degree or HND in event management or music industry management, while others work for a record company, music venue or festival organisation. Getting involved in promoting and arranging school concerts or local gigs will help you work out if this is a job you might like to do.

PROFESSIONAL VIEWPOINT
'We work in a large variety of venues, to secure the very highest calibre of local, national and international artists for the region. Having a positive impact on a local artistic community is one of the tangible benefits of this career.'
Carlo Solazzo, promoter

Promoters use their musical knowledge to help decide which musical acts will be popular with live audiences. They secure venues for shows or a location where temporary venues will be set up. Promoters use a range of media to inform the public about the festival, and organise ticket prices and sales. They may get involved in anything from making sure a band gets the food they like to hiring toilets and lighting!

↑ Festival promotion involves not only acts on the main stage but also street performers who add to the atmosphere and broad appeal of a festival.

Community musician

Community musicians may work in a variety of indoor settings, such as libraries and youth centres, or on outdoor projects such as street carnivals.

Do you think you could use your musical skills to improve people's quality of life? If so, you might like to be a community musician. These musicians collaborate with a wide variety of local groups, especially the more vulnerable or disadvantaged members of the community, encouraging music making.

Job description

Community musicians:

- work with specific communities to identify areas of musical need
- develop new ideas for community music projects
- advise and support community groups on how to increase music participation
- raise funds or apply for grants for projects
- collaborate with social workers, youth workers, teachers, arts agencies and other groups in the community to achieve successful projects
- co-ordinate and manage projects.

Different types of community musician

Work can be very varied for community musicians. One week they might lead a band workshop in a day care centre for adults with learning difficulties, to encourage communication and teamwork skills. The next week, they may be setting up a community choir in a rural village. Some community musicians work for a particular organisation in one community, or focus on just one group – perhaps the elderly or people with disabilities. However, most of them are freelancers who take on a range of work in different settings.

What skills do I need?

You can take a music degree or a course specifically designed to train you to work in the community. You will need excellent communication, teamwork and administrative skills, as well as knowledge of improvisation, composition or songwriting. Many community musicians are self-employed so they also need to be self-motivated and good at dealing with finances.

PROFESSIONAL VIEWPOINT

'Community music can happen anywhere, everyone's input is valued and nobody is excluded. It puts equal opportunities into practice, making sure that everyone has equal access and the opportunity to participate in music making no matter what their situation or background.'

Annelies de Bruine, community music development worker

↑ Setting up a community choir can get people of many different abilities and backgrounds involved in making music together.

Music journalist

Are you passionate about keeping up with the latest music releases, gigs or equipment, and communicating with others about it all? Do you have strong views about what music is good or bad? Then you might like to become a music journalist or critic, writing articles, reviews and interviews.

Music journalists attend concerts and get recordings for free. They meet musicians and others in the music business and hear the latest news first.

Job description

Music journalists:

- read press material and listen to sample CDs of new releases from record companies and artist managers
- arrange interviews (either by phone or in person) to obtain more background information on musicians or their work
- attend shows, concerts and festivals
- test musical equipment
- write and edit articles
- collaborate with photographers or picture agencies to illustrate articles or reviews
- complete reviews within publication deadlines and word limits.

Different types of music journalist

Some write for magazines, websites and blogs, while others write for radio stations, TV shows, specialist music magazines and newspapers. They may specialise in one genre, such as jazz or metal, but they usually cover a broader range of styles. In addition to reviewing concerts, new recordings and new equipment, a journalist may interview musicians and write or speak on broader topics, such as new trends in music or the music industry.

PROFESSIONAL VIEWPOINT

'To succeed, you need to know a little bit about all kinds of music and music-related topics – radio hits, Elvis, Norwegian death metal, rap, country, record labels... Well-rounded knowledge is essential if you want readers to trust your opinions. You need to be a virtual walking encyclopedia of music facts.'
Scott, music magazine reviewer

What skills do I need?

A music critic should not only be a good writer, but also an effective communicator and interviewer. They should be familiar with different types of music and have a good knowledge of music history and notable musicians, as well as keeping up to date with upcoming artists and newly released songs. Many reviewers have specialist musical knowledge gained through a degree in a music-related field, such as music theory or musical performance, or a qualification in journalism.

→ Most music journalists work flexible hours and many write their reviews from home.

Recording engineer

Most musicians could not produce high-quality CDs and radio broadcasts without recording engineers. These technicians use electronic equipment to record, mix, edit and reproduce music for stage, film, sound recordings, radio, TV and CDs.

← You may spend many hours working on a mixing desk, making fine adjustments to sounds to ensure that you get the best possible recorded tracks.

Recording engineers set up microphones and other equipment on stage or in a recording studio to capture instruments and vocals, and to mask any other sounds at the location. They record music tracks using computer software, often requesting further takes until the best performance is achieved. Then they adjust sound levels, edit out errors and mix a final master track that can be released or broadcast.

What skills do I need?

Recording engineers should have a subtle appreciation of details such as pitch and rhythm in music, and enough patience to create the highest-quality results. They need to use a lot of complicated equipment, so most recording engineers take a music technology, audio engineering or sound production course at college or university. They may then become assistants to recording engineers in order to gain hands-on experience. You can get a head start by trying to do your own recording, perhaps for school shows or community radio, or at home, and learning about current music and recording technology.

A good recording is a technical and artistic collaboration that is co-ordinated by a recording engineer.

Job description

Recording engineers:

- plan and co-ordinate recording sessions with record producers and musicians
- set up recording equipment and adjust sound levels and qualities
- operate computer recording, mixing, mastering, sequencing and sampling equipment
- listen to and balance sound levels of individual tracks in liaison with musicians and record companies
- combine tracks to produce a final master for release
- archive recordings and details for the studio.

Sound technician

When you go to a gig, you hear a rich blend of instruments and voices because a sound technician has done their job well. They make sure the audience hears the band in the best possible way, in a live (rather than recorded) setting.

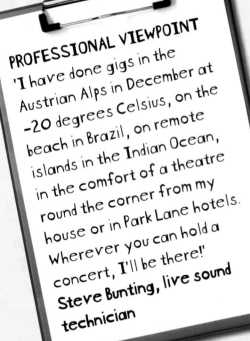

PROFESSIONAL VIEWPOINT

'I have done gigs in the Austrian Alps in December at –20 degrees Celsius, on the beach in Brazil, on remote islands in the Indian Ocean, in the comfort of a theatre round the corner from my house or in Park Lane hotels. Wherever you can hold a concert, I'll be there!'

Steve Bunting, live sound technician

Sound technicians adjust microphone levels, using a mixing desk, before and during live gigs.

Like recording engineers, sound technicians set up equipment and convert sounds entering microphones into mixes, which are heard by the audience through loudspeakers. They also create mixes for band members to hear, through on-stage or in-ear monitors, so none of the instruments is too loud. Sound requirements vary, as each auditorium has its own acoustics, depending on size, the softness or hardness of building and furnishing materials used, temperature and how many people are in the audience. Some sound technicians work on local gigs in small venues, while others travel the world doing the sound for big concerts and festivals.

What skills do I need?

You should be interested in the science of sound, including how hearing works and how people perceive sounds. You can learn a lot of what you need to know on the job, and experience is really important. However, many sound technicians have a degree in sound production, technical theatre or even physics, which gives them detailed knowledge of mixing sounds in different settings that is reinforced through experience.

Job description

Sound technicians:

- set up the stage and equipment at a venue before the band arrives
- liaise with equipment suppliers and other technicians
- carry out sound checks with bands to ensure that each microphone suits each performer
- check and create mixes to the band's or performer's specification
- monitor and adjust the mixes to make sure they are consistent during the show.

→ A sound check is vital to ensure that the audience and the performers can hear music properly and enjoyably.

Music manager

Talented as they might be, some musicians would not be as famous as they are today without a good manager. Managers, or agents, in the music industry promote, plan and co-ordinate an artist's or band's career.

What skills do I need?

You have to be passionate about the musicians you manage and determined to help them progress in their careers. Some managers start by promoting or helping out a band or artist they know, perhaps booking local gigs in pubs and small-scale festivals, even if it means working for free. Others approach a management company, seeking an internship opportunity. About half of music managers have a degree – for example, in business or communications, or a music management qualification.

↑ Managers make sure their acts are seen at major music industry events such as award ceremonies and on TV.

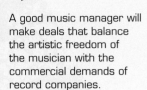

→ A good music manager will make deals that balance the artistic freedom of the musician with the commercial demands of record companies.

Different types of music manager

Some managers handle new bands without record deals. They do a lot of calling and pitching for opportunities to meet record companies, do interviews and get the music more widely known. The manager negotiates recording contracts and appearance fees. A music manager of a well-established band may organise anything from tour venues and hotels to store openings and record signing sessions, so the band can focus on the creative side of things. Top managers may co-ordinate a large team of different people handling bookings, sales, and press and media.

Job description

Music managers:
- organise musicians' lives, from travel to gigs
- send out demo CDs to record companies, radio stations and online publications
- arrange interviews with the press
- book gigs and invite record label representatives and the media to attend
- liaise with producers, festival promoters and record companies
- help book studio time and practice sessions
- draw up contracts and negotiate fees for musicians
- organise tours and promotional work.

Composer

From 'Happy Birthday' to Beethoven's 5th Symphony, composers create original, distinctive and memorable pieces of music. The compositions may be in any style (such as classical, opera, blues or brass band), and they may be performed by soloists, ensembles or huge orchestras.

→

Some composers write scores out by hand, but many input notes via a keyboard into computer programs to generate scores that they can edit more easily.

Job description

Composers:

- seek commissions, discuss composition briefs and negotiate fees
- plan an outline of the piece, including rough themes and key sounds
- write the rough score, often using a keyboard, computer software and synthesisers, to agreed deadlines
- edit and amend the score to match the brief
- prepare detailed scores for the individual musicians and instruments, or commission arrangers and copyists to do so.

Different types of composer

Composers write music for live performance on stage, but also for films, computer games and other media. Jingle writers write short, catchy tunes for radio, TV and online adverts. Arrangers adapt an existing piece of music for a particular performer or ensemble by adding accompaniments, varying rhythms and melodies. Songwriters create lyrics and music mostly for pop musicians. Almost all composers are freelancers who write to commission, such as for a new album. Many of them also perform.

What skills do I need?

A good composer is creative, original, versatile, willing to collaborate, and plays several instruments. They need a wide knowledge of compositional technique such as orchestration and harmony, and musical genres. Composers usually have a high standard of performance and music theory qualifications. Many will have gone to a specialist music college, following modules or specialisms in composition. It is important to build up a portfolio of compositions of various styles, for different-sized ensembles and genres, to show potential clients your versatility and range.

PROFESSIONAL VIEWPOINT

'Composing for theatre or film is about finding a language. I'm looking for a way to bring out what's happening in the drama through the music. I use the skills I developed as a performing musician when I'm composing. I'm lucky that I've studied music and have the skills to notate things.'

Arun Ghosh, theatre composer

↑ Inspiration for compositions can come at any time. Make sure you jot down your ideas so you don't forget them.

Music teacher

A good music teacher paces their lessons according to the pupil's abilities.

Do you have the patience, practical skills and enthusiasm to inspire others to play and compose music? Music teachers provide lessons for people of all ages. These lessons may cover general musical theory, specific instrumental training and performance techniques.

PROFESSIONAL VIEWPOINT

'I found I had a natural ability to communicate with young people. Some of my students have gone on to be professional musicians. Many others have gone down different paths, but music has given them confidence and performing skills that have helped them in whatever field they have entered.'

Liz Mummery, music teacher

Music teachers:

- plan lessons using up-to-date musical material
- assess students' ability and attainment
- teach students how to read music, play instruments and use music technology
- prepare students for music exams
- give students and parents detailed and constructive feedback
- advise on choice of instruments
- help arrange public performances for students
- update and extend their own musical knowledge and teaching skills.

What skills do I need?

Apart from good musical knowledge, a music teacher needs to be able to communicate effectively and inspire students to learn. Most music teachers hold a degree in a relevant subject or a diploma from a music college. In order to gain a place on a music course, you will usually need impressive GCSE grades as well as a music A-level. Experience is useful so try to help out at local schools with music lessons or help organise local concerts. You will need to drive if you teach individuals at their homes or travel to different places to teach.

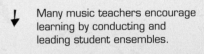
Many music teachers encourage learning by conducting and leading student ensembles.

A&R rep

An A&R rep is an Artist and Repertoire representative. This means that they work for a record company and are responsible for finding new musical talent for the company's record label. They might also find songs for artists who are already signed to the label, and liaise between the artist and the label.

What skills do I need?

You need to keep in touch with current trends so that you can spot 'the next big thing'. You also need very good persuasive powers to get bands to sign a contract with your label, and be able to communicate professionally and enthusiastically with people in the music industry. Many A&R reps have a degree in music business, music merchandising, marketing or public relations. But to begin with, most will take any position in a record company, where they can start networking before joining the A&R department.

→

A&R reps may have to listen to thousands of songs before they hear an act they want to sign up.

← Adele wins an Oscar for best original song in 2013. Her rapid rise to stardom has been helped by the A&R marketing work of her label, XL Recordings.

Job description

A&R reps:
• seek new artists – for example, through gigs, demos and contact with music managers and festival promoters
• contact artists who are with competing record labels when their contracts are due to expire
• sign new talent, with executive approval
• negotiate record deals with artists and their managers
• help find new material for their artists to record
• market new records.

A&R reps find artists by going to lots of gigs and listening to hundreds of demos. They seek information on the Internet about promising artists, using search engines, fan pages, and all types of social media. Once they have negotiated record deals with musicians and their managers, A&R reps usually help artists find new material that they think will be popular. They market their recordings through contacts at radio stations and through album launch events.

DJ

They might be playing other people's music, but DJs (disc jockeys) put on performances of their own. They select, play and introduce recorded music for audiences on the radio or at live venues.

↑ Watch DJs at work whenever you can. See how they construct their shows and how they manage the crowd. After the show, ask for a few tips. Most DJs will be happy to give you advice if they know you're serious.

Job description

DJs:
- know their audience, and what type of music they want, before an event or show
- play music on vinyl, CDs or digital MP3s, using equipment including turntables, mixers and headphones
- choose music to be played and plan how it will be blended into a programme
- keep up an entertaining and natural flow of songs and chat
- interact with the audience – for example, through phone-ins and playing requests
- plan future shows by preparing scripts and playlists.

What skills do I need?

You need to be confident about speaking and performing live in front of an audience, so it helps to get involved with drama or debating clubs at school and have a go at DJ-ing for friends' parties or a youth club to get experience. Some DJs study DJ-ing or music production at college or go to radio or broadcasting schools.

Different types of DJ

Some DJs introduce and play separate tracks to audiences. They may specialise in particular genres or periods of music, such as 70s disco or world music, or play a wide variety. Other DJs create selections to back live performers (including MCs or rappers or instrumentalists), using multiple turntables and digital samples. Others create programmes for radio stations, locally or nationally.

PROFESSIONAL VIEWPOINT
'Show what you can do. Get into hospital radio or track down a local station that comes on air for a few hours a week. The radio authority can tell you your local station. Send tapes, but be yourself and show you can hold an audience's attention.'
Tracy Jones, BBC radio presenter

← Many aspiring radio DJs take an intern position at a local radio station or a college radio station to see if they like the work.

Instrument technician

Do you find yourself staring at the construction of your instrument, when you could be playing it, and imagining how you could make improvements to its sound? If so, perhaps you should be an instrument technician who designs, makes, repairs, maintains and restores musical instruments.

Different types of instrument technician

As the work is highly skilled, technicians usually specialise in particular instruments such as keyboards, string or woodwind instruments. Some technicians only build new guitars and basses, while others reproduce and restore period instruments, like harpsichords. Some technicians work for companies that make, sell or repair musical instruments, while a few are employed by famous bands while they are on tour.

↑ Musicians can get the best out of instruments if they are regularly tuned and maintained.

What skills do I need?

Instrument technicians need to be practical, have an eye for detail and be good at making and repairing things. Woodworking, metalworking and electronics skills are very useful. You need an ear for tuning and tone, and patience because some of the work (such as finishing fine instruments to a high standard) takes a long time. Some technicians train with an employer and learn in their workshop, and others do instrument technology or makers' and repairers' courses that cover topics including acoustics, instrument design and history, and restoration techniques.

Instrument technicians:

- design instruments to their own or clients' briefs
- source the right materials, such as types of wood, metal and plastic, and electronics
- use a variety of hand and machine tools and construction methods to make new instruments
- upgrade parts of instruments, and replace or repair damaged or worn parts
- use finishing techniques such as cleaning and varnishing
- tune and restring instruments.

↓ A technician designs the shape of an electric guitar. Many technicians get their enthusiasm for making and repairing instruments because they play themselves.

PROFESSIONAL VIEWPOINT

'I'd always enjoyed tinkering with instruments: changing parts and generally trying to improve them. When I realised I needed to further my learning, I went to university, gaining a BA (Hons) in Musical Instrument Making and Repair. Always buy cheap broken guitars and practise repairing them before you let yourself loose on a £2,000 guitar.'

Richard Meyrick, musical instrument maker

Glossary

acoustics how clearly the sound is heard; the quality of sound

administrative relating to the running of a business

advertising communication through words and design, intended to draw attention to a product, service or cause

amplifier device that increases the volume of sound

archive to store something in a collection

audition sample performance – for example, by a singer or musician

balance relative volume of different instruments or sounds in a recording

broadcasting business of making and transmitting TV and radio programmes

commission an arrangement whereby something, such as a song or piece of music, is produced in return for payment

demo recording used to demonstrate a music artist or their songs or both

edit to check, improve and prepare a work for publication or release

ensemble group of musicians, actors or dancers who perform together

freelancer someone who works independently on paid jobs for different employers

internship time spent working for an employer to learn skills needed for a job

liaise to talk to or communicate with people so they can work together

marketing finding out what people want to buy and how to sell things to them

master an original recording, movie, or document, from which copies can be made

media the Internet, newspapers, magazines, television, and other means of passing on information to the public

merchandising making and selling products used to promote a particular band, artist or movie

mix blend of output that balances different sources of music

monitor device used to check sound

motor control co-ordination of nerves, muscles and bones to produce movements

musical genre type or style of music, such as jazz or classical

pitching trying to persuade someone to buy or accept something

portfolio collection of creative works assembled to display the skills of a musician or other artist

public relations work that creates a favourable public image of a person, product or service

publicise advertise, draw attention to

sampling technique of digitally encoding music or sound and reusing it as part of a composition or recording

score written form or notation of music

self-employed working for oneself rather than for another person or company

sequencing repetition of a musical phrase or melody at a higher or lower pitch

session musician musician or singer who works with others at live performances or recording sessions

sound check short session when a sound engineer tests the quality of musical sound

Further information

There are many specific courses, apprenticeships and jobs using music skills, so where do you go to find out more? It is really useful to meet up with careers advisers at school or college and to attend careers fairs to see the range of opportunities. Remember that public libraries and newspapers are other important sources of information. The earlier you check out your options, the better prepared you will be to put your musical skills to good use as you earn a living in future.

Books

Careers in Music, Sara Peacock, Rhinegold Education, 2013

Cool Jobs in the Music Business, Jeffrey Rabhan, In Tune; Pap/DVD edition, 2012

DJing (Master This!), Matt Anniss, Wayland, 2012

Guitar (Master This!), Seb Wesson, Wayland, 2011

Music (Jobs If You Like…), Charlotte Guillain, Raintree, 2013

Performing Live (The Music Scene), Matt Anniss, Franklin Watts, 2012

Top Jobs: Being a DJ (Radar), Lisa Regan and Matt Anniss, Wayland, 2012

Websites

www.creative-choices.co.uk/industry-insight/inside/music
This website has some interesting career insights from people working in music, including tips on how to get into their careers.

www.bbc.co.uk/programmes/p010j8y5/profiles/advice-for-unsigned-and-undiscovered-musicians
How would you go about getting a recording contract if no one but your family and pets has heard your music?! Visit this website to find out.

www.bbc.co.uk/programmes/p016hxsl
Watch some short videos of people with musical skills talking about live performance.

www.recordproduction.com/
Meet a wide range of successful record producers and recording engineers.

Index

I'M GOOD AT...

Contents of all the titles in the series:

WAYLAND